Half You Heard of FRACTIONS?

by Thomas K. and Heather Adamson

Consultant:
Tamara Olson, Associate Professor
Department of Mathematical Sciences
Michigan Technological University

CAPSTONE PRESS
a capstone imprint

A+ Books are published by Capstone Press,
1710 Roe Crest Drive, North Mankato, Minnesota 56003.
www.capstonepub.com

 Books published by Capstone Press are manufactured with paper
containing at least 10 percent post-consumer waste.

Library of Congress Cataloging-in-Publication Data
Cataloging-in-publication information is on file with the Library of Congress.
ISBN 978-1-4296-7556-7 (hardcover)
ISBN 9781-14296-7860-5 (paperback)

Credits
Kristen Mohn, editor; Gene Bentdahl, designer; Svetlana Zhurkin, media researcher; Laura Manthe,
 production specialist; Sarah Schuette, photo stylist; Marcy Morin, studio scheduler

Photo Credits
All photos by Capstone Studio/Karon Dubke

Note to Parents, Teachers, and Librarians
This Fun with Numbers book uses photos of everyday objects in a nonfiction format to introduce
the concept of fractions, including halves, thirds, quarters, wholes, numerators and denominators,
and daily applications of fractions. *Half You Heard of Fractions?* is designed to be read aloud to a
pre-reader or to be read independently by an early reader. The book encourages further learning
by including the following sections: Table of Contents, Taking It Further, Read More, and Internet
Sites. Early readers may need assistance using these features.

Printed in the United States of America in North Mankato, Minnesota.
102011   006405CGS12

TABLE of CONTENTS

What Are Fractions?

Ready, set, go! Carly and Ava are racing around the track. Carly is in the lead, but it isn't over yet! They've only completed a fraction of the race.

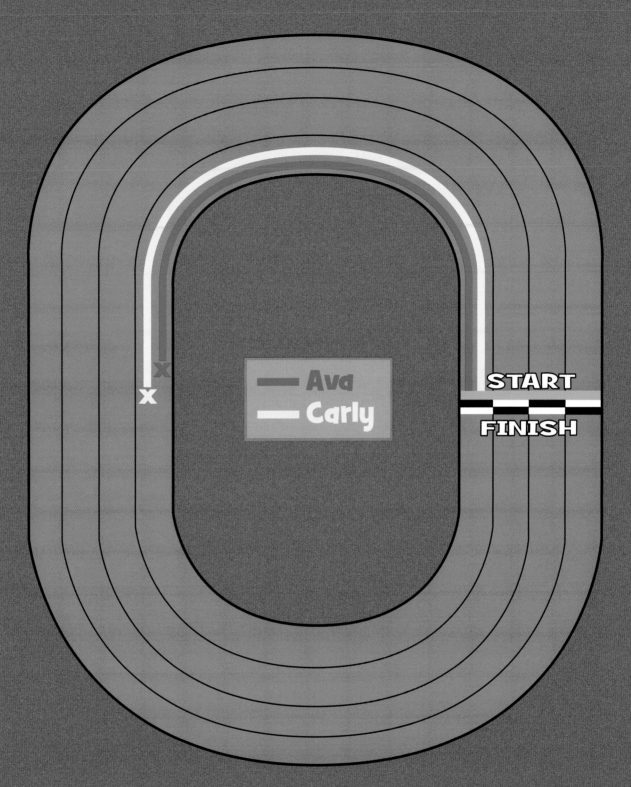

Fraction means part of a whole. We can
use fractions to describe how much.
Half the race is done. Half is a fraction.

Fractions can make sure everyone gets a fair share. Fractions divide things into equal parts.

6

An apple can be split into two pieces that are the same size. There is still the same total amount of apple, but now it's ready to share. Each person gets a fraction of the apple—one-half.

A fraction is shown as two numbers with a line between them. The top number, the numerator, tells how many parts are being counted. The bottom number, the denominator, tells how many parts make up the whole thing.

Write It	Say It	See It
1/2, $\frac{1}{2}$	one-half	
1/4, $\frac{1}{4}$	one-fourth or one-quarter	
3/4, $\frac{3}{4}$	three-fourths or three-quarters	
1/5, $\frac{1}{5}$	one-fifth	
3/7, $\frac{3}{7}$	three-sevenths	
9/10, $\frac{9}{10}$	nine-tenths	
2/3, $\frac{2}{3}$	two-thirds	

Anything you can count or measure can be made into a fraction. There are eight kids at the party. Five are girls. As a fraction, 5/8 of the children are girls.

How many are boys? 3/8 are boys.
There are more girls than boys at the party.
5/8 is more than 3/8.

Parts of a Whole

Folding can show us parts of a whole. Unfold a napkin. Do you see the sections? This one has four equal parts. 4/4 is how you would show that as a fraction.

A fraction with the same numerator and denominator equals one whole, or 1. All of the parts are being counted.

Now fold the napkin in half. Two squares are showing. 2/4 is the same as 1/2. These are different names for the same fraction.

1/4

1/4 = 2/4

2/4 = 1/2

Sam and Kyla are going to make trail mix. They need cereal, raisins, and peanuts. The recipe says the mix is:

- 2 parts cereal   = $2/4$

- 1 part raisins   = $1/4$

- 1 part peanuts   = $1/4$

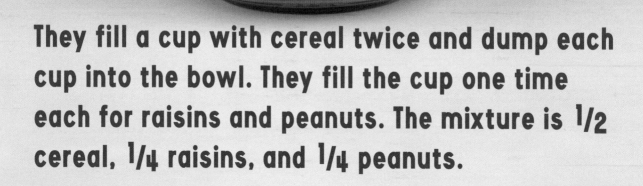

They fill a cup with cereal twice and dump each cup into the bowl. They fill the cup one time each for raisins and peanuts. The mixture is $1/2$ cereal, $1/4$ raisins, and $1/4$ peanuts.

14

"Let's add chocolate chips!"

If Sam and Kyla added one cup of chocolate chips, the recipe would have five parts instead of four. What fraction would the chocolate chips be?

Juan and Mick each have a list of chores to do. Juan finished three of his six chores. He is half done with his work. 3/6 is one-half.

Juan's list:

½
- ✔ make bed
- ✔ empty garbage
- ✔ practice piano

½
- walk dog
- pick up toys
- fold laundry

$3/6 = 1/2$

Mick has two of his six chores done. He has only finished one-third of his work. 2/6 is one-third of the whole list.

Mick's list:

1/3
✔ wash dishes
✔ study spelling

1/3
feed fish
sort recycling

1/3
sweep floor
vacuum rugs

$$2/6 = 1/3$$

Friendly Fractions

You can divide licorice to share.

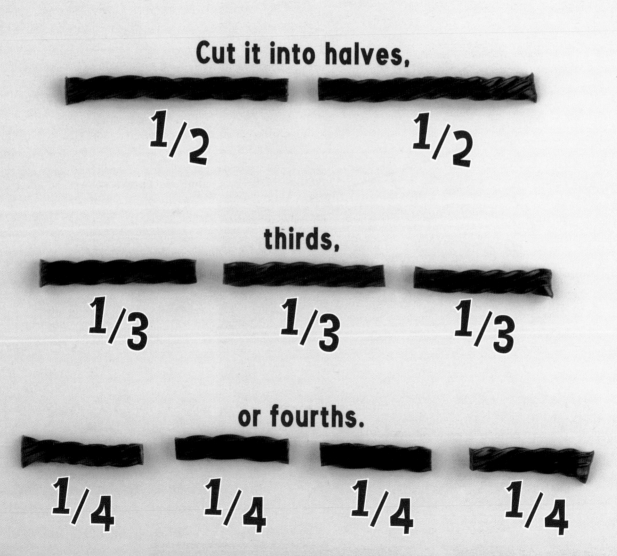

1

Cut it into halves,

1/2   1/2

thirds,

1/3   1/3   1/3

or fourths.

1/4   1/4   1/4   1/4

The pieces get smaller when you make more parts.

Let's compare sizes. Would you rather have 1/4 or 1/2 of the licorice rope? Don't let the larger denominator fool you!

Look at the size of the fourth. It's shorter than the half. It takes two of the fourths to be as long as one half.

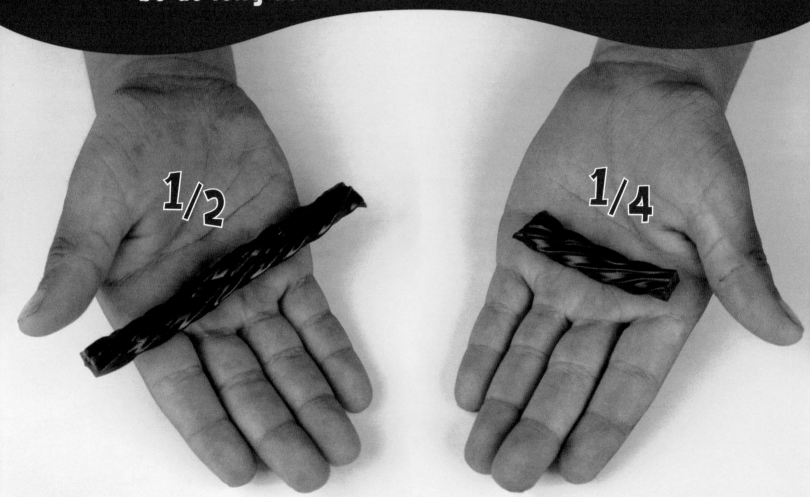

How about one-third? Is 1/3 smaller or larger than 1/4?

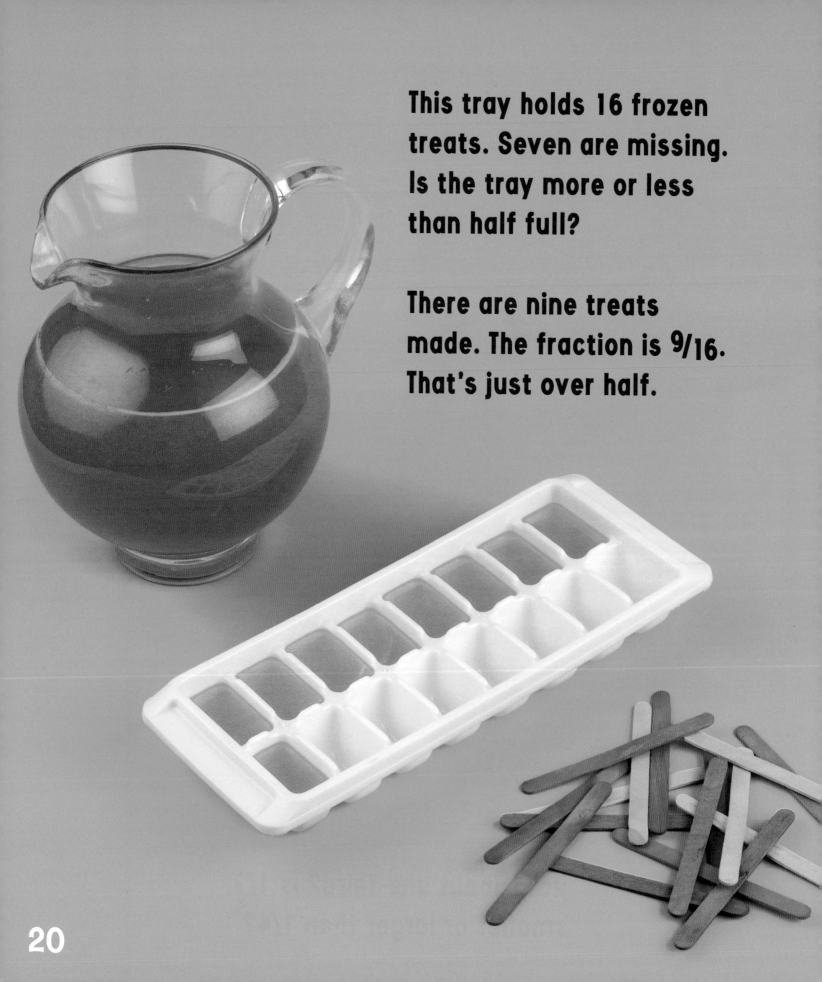

This tray holds 16 frozen treats. Seven are missing. Is the tray more or less than half full?

There are nine treats made. The fraction is 9/16. That's just over half.

Now the tray is ⁷/₁₆ full. Is it missing more than half of its treats? How many treats equal half of the tray? Quick, before they melt!

Fractions in Action

Lots of things use fractions. Rulers show measurements in fractions. The smaller lines are equal parts of an inch. This car is 4 and 3/4, or 4 3/4, inches long.

$4\frac{3}{4}$

Money can be measured in fractions. A quarter coin gets its name because it is one-quarter of a dollar. What fraction of a dollar is a dime? Here's a hint: There are 10 dimes in one dollar.

$\frac{1}{4}$ dollar

$\frac{1}{?}$ dollar

Even games are measured with fractions. A basketball game has four quarters. The game is divided into four equal parts.

Each half has two quarters.
Two quarters out of four is
half the game. It's halftime!

Clocks can show fractions too.
A clock shows parts of an hour.

This clock shows the minute hand 1/4 of the way around. Another way to say 1/4 is "a quarter." It's a quarter after seven.

On this clock the minute hand is halfway around. It's half past seven.

What fraction of an hour does this clock show? Don't be late!

Fractions are all around us. Twenty-five cents is 1/4 of a dollar. A slice of pizza is 1/8 of the pizza. One time around the track can make a whole race. Carly was faster for the first half. But Ava pulled ahead in the second half. Those are fractions in action! Good race!

CHECK YOUR FRACTIONS

Page 15:
If there are five cups of ingredients total, the denominator would be five. One cup of chocolate chips would equal 1/5.

Page 19:
1/3 is larger than 1/4.

Page 21:
The tray is missing more than half its treats. There are 16 sections. Eight is half of 16. 8/16 is the same as ½, or one-half.

Page 23:
There are 10 dimes in one dollar, so a dime is 1/10 of a dollar.

Page 27:
This clock shows the fraction ¾. The minute hand has traveled ¾ of the way around the hour.

TAKING IT FURTHER

Look for fractions at the store. If something is half price, how much will it cost? Look for containers that are divided into fractions. You can buy one whole jar of applesauce. Or you can buy a package of six cups of applesauce. If you eat one cup, what fraction is left?

You can divide a piece of paper into fractions by folding it. Fold the paper in half to make two halves. Fold it again to make four fourths. Cut along the folds to make equal parts.

Look back at pages 18 and 19. What happens if you cut the whole licorice into 10 pieces? What fraction would three of those pieces be? What if you cut the whole into 50 pieces and took one piece? What fraction is that?

GLOSSARY

compare—to look closely at things in order to discover ways they are alike or different

denominator—the bottom number in a fraction that shows how many equal parts the whole number can be divided into

divide—to separate into parts or groups

equal—being the same in amount

fraction—one or more equal parts of a whole

numerator—the top number in a fraction that shows how many equal parts of the denominator are being counted

READ MORE

Adler, David A. *Working with Fractions.* New York: Holiday House, 2007.

Allen, Nancy. *What's a Fraction?* Little World Math. Vero Beach, Fla: Rourke Pub., 2011.

Speed Shaskan, Trisha. *If You Were a Fraction.* Math Fun. Minneapolis: Picture Window Books, 2009.

INTERNET SITES

FactHound offers a safe, fun way to find Internet sites related to this book. All of the sites on FactHound have been researched by our staff.

Here's all you do:

Visit www.facthound.com

Type in this code: 9781429675567

Super-cool stuff! Check out projects, games and lots more at
www.capstonekids.com